Speaking *of* Art

Colorful Quotes by Famous Painters

EDITED BY

BOB

RACZKA

M Millbrook Press/Minneapolis

"The only time I feel alive is when I'm painting."

—VINCENT VAN GOGH

The Sower

Vincent van Gogh

1888

Kröller-Müller Museum,
Otterlo, Netherlands

Howling Dog

Paul Klee

1928

Minneapolis Institute of Arts,
Minnesota

"**A line is a dot that goes for a walk.**"

—Paul Klee

"Good color sings. It is melodious, aroma-like, never over-baked."

—HENRI MATISSE

> **"**I always pet a dog with my left hand because if he bit me I'd still have my right hand to paint with."
> —JUAN GRIS

Landscape with Houses at Ceret

Juan Gris

1913

Galeria Theo, Madrid, Spain

A Beautiful World

Grandma Moses
(Anna Mary Robertson Moses)

1948

Galerie St. Etienne,
New York

" **If I didn't start paintIng, I would have raised chickens.** "

—GRANDMA MOSES

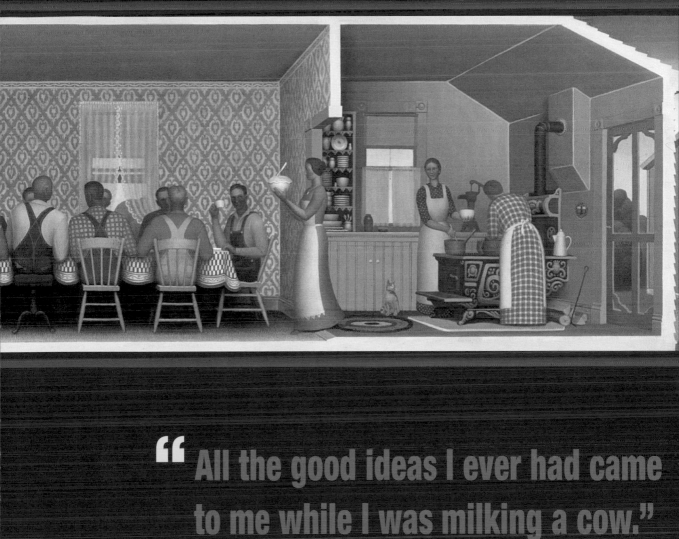

"All the good ideas I ever had came to me while I was milking a cow."

—GRANT WOOD

*Lady Agnew
of Lochnaw*

John Singer
Sargent

1892

National
Gallery of
Scotland,
Edinburgh,
Scotland

"A portrait is a picture in which there is just a tiny little something not quite right about the mouth."

—JOHN SINGER SARGENT

"I paint self-portraits because I am so often alone, because I am the person I know the best."

—FRIDA KAHLO

Self-Portrait with Monkey

Frida Kahlo

1938

Albright-Knox Art Gallery, Buffalo, New York

"**If [painting] weren't so difficult, it wouldn't be fun.**"
—EDGAR DEGAS

The Rehearsal

Edgar Degas

ca. 1878–1879

The Frick Collection,
New York

Three flags

Jasper Johns

1958

Whitney Museum of American Art,
New York

"Take an object. Do something to it. Do something else to it."

—JASPER JOHNS

"Painting is no problem; the problem is what to do when you're not painting."

—JACKSON POLLOCK

"I found I could say things with color and shapes that I couldn't say any other way—things I had no words for."

—GEORGIA O'KEEFFE

Evening Star No. III

"I try to apply colors like words that shape poems, like notes that shape music."
—Joan Miró

The Poetess

Joan Miró

1940

Colin Collection, New York

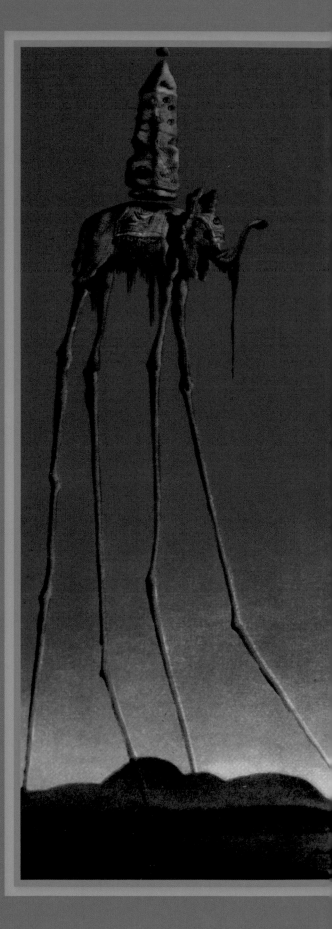

The Elephants

Salvador Dalí

1948

Gala–Salvador Dalí Foundation,
Figueres, Spain

"People love
mystery,
and that is
why they
love my
paintings."
—SALVADOR DALÍ

Bouquet with Flying Lovers

Marc Chagall

ca. 1934–1947

Tate Gallery,
London,
England

"**Art must be an expression of love or it is nothing."**

—MARC CHAGALL

"Art is the soul of people."
—ROMARE BEARDEN

Family

Romare Bearden

1986

Smithsonian
American
Art Museum,
Washington, D.C.

Untitled

Keith Haring

1986

Keith Haring Foundation,
New York

"My contribution to the world is my ability to draw. I will draw as much as I can for as many people as I can for as long as I can."

—KEITH HARING

Interior with a Girl Drawing

Pablo Picasso

1935

The Museum of Modern Art,
New York

"**To draw, you must close your eyes and sing.**"

—PABLO PICASSO

COLORFUL FACTS
about the ARTISTS

Grandma Moses (1860–1961) *American*
Anna Mary Robertson Moses was born in upstate New York, where she lived most of her life. A self-taught folk artist, Anna began painting in her seventies. She painted scenes from rural life, making more than thirty-six hundred paintings in three decades. Before becoming famous, Anna sold small paintings for $2 and large ones for $3. In 2006 one of her paintings sold for $1.2 million. She lived to be 101.

Vincent van Gogh (1853–1890) *Dutch*
Exactly one year before Vincent was born, his parents had a baby who died at birth. His name was also Vincent van Gogh. Before becoming a painter, Vincent worked as an art dealer, a teacher, a bookstore clerk, and a missionary. When he was twenty-seven, Vincent's younger brother and best friend, Theo, suggested that he become an artist. During the next ten years, Vincent created nearly nine hundred paintings.

Grant Wood (1891–1942) *American*
Born in Iowa, Grant studied art in Minneapolis, Minnesota, and at Chicago's Art Institute in Illinois. He also made four trips to Europe, where he was influenced by the Dutch painter Jan van Eyck. Grant rejected the abstract art of Europe, preferring to paint scenes of rural life in the American Midwest. He even dressed in farmer's overalls when he was photographed. Like Paul Klee, Grant painted camouflage on U.S. Army tanks and cannons during World War I.

Paul Klee (1879–1940) *German/Swiss*
Paul was born near Bern, Switzerland. As a boy, he loved music and started playing the violin when he was seven. He also loved art—especially drawing in his schoolbooks! As a young man, he studied art in Munich, Germany, and later taught at the Bauhaus, a famous art school. In all, he created nearly nine thousand works of art. During World War I (1914–1918), Paul even painted camouflage on German airplanes.

John Singer Sargent (1856–1925)
American expatriate
Before John was born, his parents left the United States to live in Europe. As a result, John was born in Florence, Italy, and grew up traveling. The most successful portrait artist of his day, John painted more than nine hundred oil portraits in all, including those of President Theodore Roosevelt, author Robert Louis Stevenson, and artist Claude Monet. He rarely did sketches first, preferring to work directly with paint.

Henri Matisse (1869–1954) *French*
Henri grew up in northeastern France. At seventeen he went to Paris, France, to study law. He didn't start painting until he was nineteen, when he had a case of appendicitis and his mother gave him some art supplies to keep him busy as he recovered. Henri loved it so much, he gave up law for art. Even when he was confined to a wheelchair in his eighties, Henri made large collages with cut paper. He called this "painting with scissors."

Frida Kahlo (1907–1954) *Mexican*
Born near Mexico City, Frida contracted polio at the age of six. At eighteen she was on a bus that collided with a trolley car, breaking her spinal column, collarbone, pelvis, leg, and several ribs. Confined to a bed for three months, she painted to pass the time. Frida recovered but experienced pain for the rest of her life. Many of her fifty-five self-portraits include references to her pain. She married Diego Rivera, the Mexican muralist.

Juan Gris (1887–1927) *Spanish*
Juan's real name was José Victoriano González. Born in Madrid, Spain, he was the thirteenth child in a family of fourteen. When he was nineteen, José left school, changed his name to Juan Gris, and moved to Paris to become an artist. There he became a friend of Pablo Picasso, who taught him about Cubism, a way of seeing and painting things from many angles. Juan loved this exciting new style of painting and, using his own bright colors, made it his own.

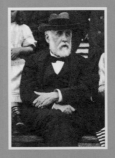

Edgar Degas (1834–1917) *French*
Edgar was born in Paris and began painting early in life. At eighteen, he had his own studio. Edgar started out as a painter of scenes from history but later became a painter of everyday life. Two of his favorite subjects were dancers and racehorses. To learn, Edgar copied paintings in the Louvre, a large art museum in Paris. At twenty-seven, he had copied more than seven hundred works of art! Edgar also loved photography, sculpture, and working in pastels.

Jasper Johns (1930–   ) *American*
Born in Georgia, Jasper was abandoned by his parents as a child and raised by relatives in South Carolina. He began drawing when he was three years old. Jasper painted *Flag*, one of his most famous works, after having a dream about the American flag. His other favorite subjects include maps, numbers, and targets. In 2006 one of his paintings sold for $80 million.

Jackson Pollock (1912–1956) *American*
Born in Wyoming, Jackson first showed an interest in art during high school. Influenced by Mexican mural painting (the art of painting on walls and ceilings) and Native American sand painting (the art of pouring colored sand onto a surface to make a painting), Jackson developed his own technique, dripping and pouring paint onto canvases laid on the floor. Many of his paintings include nails, buttons, sand, and even broken glass!

Georgia O'Keeffe (1887–1986) *American*
Georgia was born on a dairy farm in Wisconsin. Her mother believed women should be educated, so she made Georgia and her sisters take art classes as girls. By eighth grade, Georgia knew she wanted to be an artist. She went to New York City to be part of the art scene there, but late in her life, Georgia left New York for New Mexico, where she fell in love with the desert. Georgia rarely signed her paintings, but she often wrote the letters *OK* on the back.

Joan Miró (1893–1983) *Spanish*
Born near Barcelona, Spain, Joan started taking drawing classes when he was seven. He moved to Paris in 1920, where he was influenced by Surrealism, an art style based on dreams and fantasies. In addition to painting, Joan made ceramics, sculpture, murals, and more. In 1974 he created a woven tapestry for the World Trade Center in New York City. This work was destroyed in the September 11, 2001, terrorist attacks.

Salvador Dalí (1904–1989) *Spanish*
Like van Gogh, Salvador Dalí had an older brother with the same name who died before he was born. His mother, who encouraged him in his art, died when he was sixteen. All his life, Salvador enjoyed drawing attention to himself. He dressed extravagantly, acted strangely, and grew a flamboyant mustache. Best known for his bizarre paintings, Salvador also worked in movies, fashion, and photography.

Marc Chagall (1887–1985) *Russian*
Marc was born in Vitebsk, Russia, the oldest of nine children. Although his family was poor, Marc had a happy childhood. In fact, he often painted scenes from his early life. People love his paintings for their vibrant colors, but Marc also created wonderful stained glass pieces, ceramics, and even stage sets. Because he was Jewish, he had to flee to the United States from Nazi-occupied Paris during World War II (1939–1945).

Romare Bearden (1911–1988) *American*
Born in Charlotte, North Carolina, Romare became a great collage artist, but he had many talents. He created political cartoons, designed stage costumes and sets, illustrated books, and even wrote music. His song, "Sea Breeze," is a jazz classic. While in college, Romare played Negro League baseball. (During this time, the major leagues hired only white players.) Romare was offered a chance to play in the majors if he "passed for white," but he refused.

Keith Haring (1958–1990) *American*
Born in Pennsylvania, Keith loved to draw as a boy. A fan of Walt Disney and Dr. Seuss, he learned basic cartooning from his father. At twenty he moved to New York, where he was influenced by performance artists and graffiti writers. Keith became famous for drawing on unused advertising panels in the New York City subways. He went on to create public art works around the world. He died of AIDS at thirty-one.

Pablo Picasso (1881–1973) *Spanish*
As a boy, Pablo loved to draw. According to his mother, Pablo's first word was *piz*, short for *lapis*, the Spanish word for "pencil." He was trained by his father, an art professor, until he was thirteen. Pablo went on to create nearly fifty thousand works of art during his long life. For one of his most famous sculptures, the *Chicago Picasso*, he refused to be paid one hundred thousand dollars. He made the work a gift to the people of Chicago.

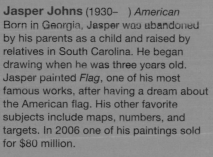

To Claire, whose art is beyond compare

Text copyright © 2010 by Bob Raczka

Millbrook Press
A division of Lerner Publishing Group, Inc.
241 First Avenue North
Minneapolis, MN 55401 U.S.A.

Website address: www.lernerbooks.com

Library of Congress Cataloging-in-Publication Data

    Speaking of art : colorful quotes by famous painters / edited by Bob Raczka.
       p. cm.
    ISBN: 978-0-7613-5054-5 (lib. bdg. : alk. paper)
    1. Art—Quotations, maxims, etc. 2. Artists—Quotations. I. Raczka, Bob.
    II. Title: Colorful quotes by famous painters.
    PN6084.A8S64 2010
    700—dc22   2009023484

Manufactured in the United States of America
1 – DP – 12/15/09

Quotation Citations

Back cover and p. 2: *The Kennedy Center ArtsEdge*, n.d., http://artsedge.kennedy-center.org/explore/qts.cfm (July 8, 2009).

p. 4: Susan Piedmont-Palladino, *Tools of the Imagination: Drawing Tools and Technologies from the Eighteenth Century to the Present* (Princeton, NJ: Princeton Architectural Press, 2006), 21.

p. 6: Hayden Herrera, *Matisse: A Portrait* (New York: Harcourt Brace, 1993), 75.

p. 7: Janine Warnod, *Washboat Days: Montmartre, Picasso and the Artists Revolution* (New York: Grossman Publishers, 1972), 204.

Front jacket flap and p. 9: Donna Ward La Cour, *Artists in Quotation: A Dictionary of the Creative Thoughts of Painters, Sculptors, Designers, Writers, Educators, and Others* (Jefferson, NC: McFarland & Company, 1989), 119.

p. 11: Richard Kenin and Justin Wintle, *The Dictionary of Biographical Quotation of British and American Subjects* (New York: Knopf, 1978), 811.

p. 12: Evan Charteris, *John Sargent* (New York: C. Scribner's Sons, 1927), 157.

p. 13: Andrea Kettenmann, *Frida Kahlo 1907-1954: Pain and Passion* (Cologne: Taschen, 1999), 18.

p. 15: La Cour, *Artists in Quotation*, 123.

p. 17: Jeffrey Weiss, *Jasper Johns: An Allegory of Painting, 1955-1965* (New Haven, CT: Yale University Press, 2007), 19.

p. 18: B. H. Friedman, *Jackson Pollock: Energy Made Visible* (New York: Da Capo, 1995), 214.

p. 19: James R. Miller, *Voices from Earth: A Book of Gentle Wisdom* (Victoria: Trafford Publishing, 2006), 29.

p. 21: Hugh Rawson and Margaret Miner, *The New International Dictionary of Quotations* (Boston: E.P. Dutton, 1986), 27.

p. 22: *The Kennedy Center ArtsEdge*, n.d., http://artsedge.kennedy-center.org/explore/qts.cfm (July 8, 2009).

p. 24: "Art Quotes and Sayings," *Sayings & Quotes*, n.d., http://www.sayingsnquotes.com/quotations-by-subject/art-quotes-and-sayings/ (August 28, 2009).

p. 25: Bill Caldwell, "Romare Bearden: Art Is the Soul of People." *Encore* 1 (October 1972): 58–61.

p. 27: Princeton Review Publishing Staff, *Guide to College Majors 2008* (Princeton, NJ: Princeton Review, 2008), 225.

p. 28: La Cour, *Artists in Quotation*, 44.